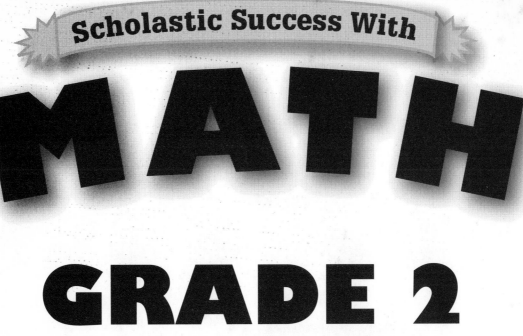

Scholastic Success With
MATH
GRADE 2

SCHOLASTIC
PROFESSIONAL BOOKS

New York ◉ Toronto ◉ London ◉ Auckland ◉ Sydney

Mexico City ◉ New Delhi ◉ Hong Kong ◉ Buenos Aires

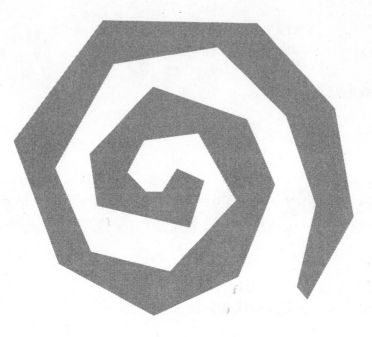

Compiled and produced by Susan L. Lingo, Bright Ideas Books™

Cover design by Maria Lilja

Cover art by Victoria Raymond

Interior design by Ellen Matlach Hassell
for Boultinghouse & Boultinghouse, Inc.

ISBN 0-439-41966-2

Printed in the U.S.A.

Contents

About the Book 4

Number Concepts 5–12
Counting, missing numbers, odd and even numbers, ordinals,
place value, greater than/less than/equal to

Shapes & Patterns 13–17
Identifying shapes, combining shapes, three-dimensional
shapes, and identifying patterns

Addition 18–25
Adding 1- and 2-digit numbers with and without regrouping, column
addition, adding 2 and 3 digits with regrouping, and missing addends

Subtraction 26–35
Relation between addition and subtraction, subtracting 1-
and 2-place numbers with and without regrouping

Multiplication & Division 36–39
Fact families, multiplication picture problems, and introducing division

Problem Solving 40–44
Sorting and grouping, solving story and picture problems,
number sentences, and writing simple equations

Time, Money, & Measurement 45–51
Telling time, comparing coins and amounts, comparing
lengths and weights, and introducing perimeter

Graphs, Charts & Tables 52–54
Ordered pairs, reading and creating simple graphs, plotting
coordinates, tally counts, and reading charts and tables

Fractions 55–59
Identifying parts of a whole and finding parts of a whole or group

Answer Key 60
Instant Skills Index 64

About the Book

"Nothing succeeds like success."
—Alexandre Dumas the Elder, 1854

And no other math resource helps kids succeed like *Scholastic Success With Math!* For classroom or at-home use, this exciting series for kids in grades 1 through 6 provides invaluable reinforcement and practice for math skills such as:

❑ number sense and concepts
❑ reasoning and logic
❑ basic operations and computations
❑ story problems and equations
❑ time, money, and measurement
❑ fractions, decimals, and percentages
❑ geometry and basic shapes
❑ graphs, charts, tables ... and more!

Each 64-page book contains loads of challenging puzzles, inviting games, and clever practice pages to keep kids delighted and excited as they strengthen their basic math skills.

What makes *Scholastic Success With Math* so solid?

Each practice page in the series reinforces a specific, age-appropriate skill as outlined in one or more of the following standardized tests:

◎ *Iowa Tests of Basic Skills*
◎ *California Tests of Basic Skills*
◎ *California Achievement Test*
◎ *Metropolitan Achievement Test*
◎ *Stanford Achievement Test*

These are the skills that help kids succeed in daily math work and on standardized achievement tests. And the handy Instant Skills Index at the back of every book helps you succeed in zeroing in on the skills your kids need most!

Take the lead and help kids succeed with *Scholastic Success With Math*.
Parents and teachers agree: No one helps kids succeed like Scholastic!

Lone Donor

Name _Grace_   Date _7\23\07_

This is a number line. The numbers increase as you go along the line.

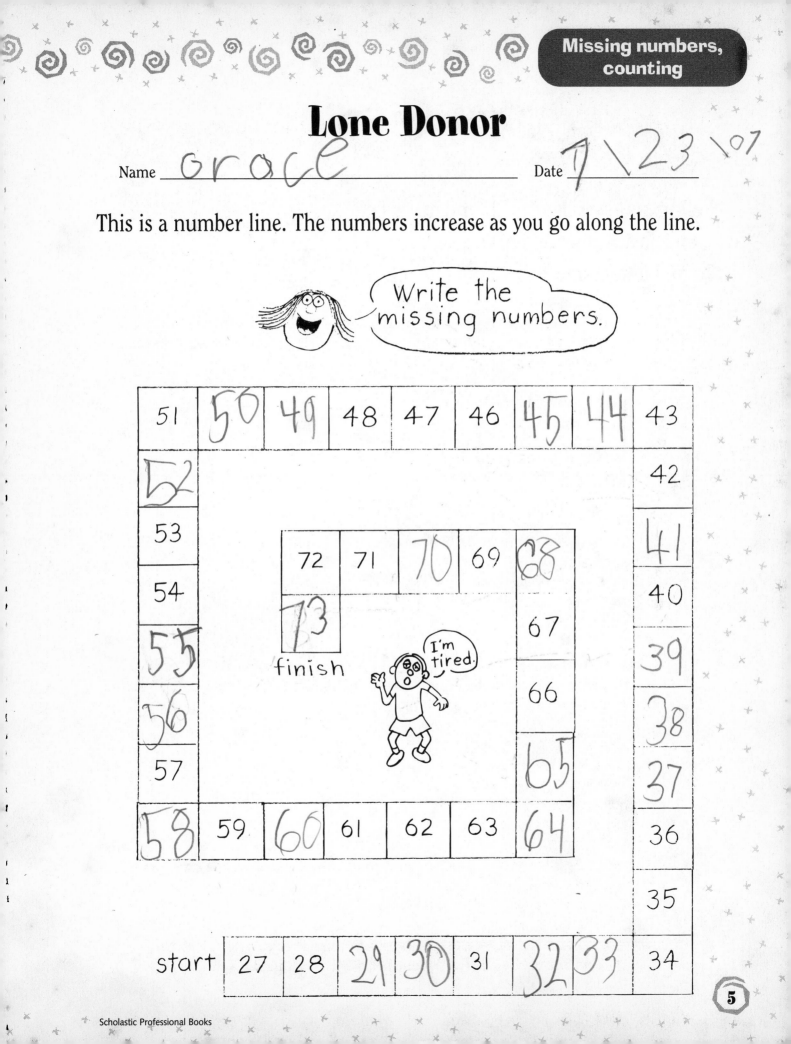

Write the missing numbers.

51	50	49	48	47	46	45	44	43

52
53
54
55
56
57

72 71 70 69 68
73 finish
67
66
65
64

I'm tired.

| 58 | 59 | 60 | 61 | 62 | 63 | 64 |

42
41
40
39
38
37
36
35
34

start | 27 | 28 | 29 | 30 | 31 | 32 | 33 | 34

Mystery Critter

Name _____ Date _____

I climb up the side of walls and never fall.

I am a fast runner and have a very long tail. Who am I? _____

To find out, connect the numbers in order from 20 to 68.

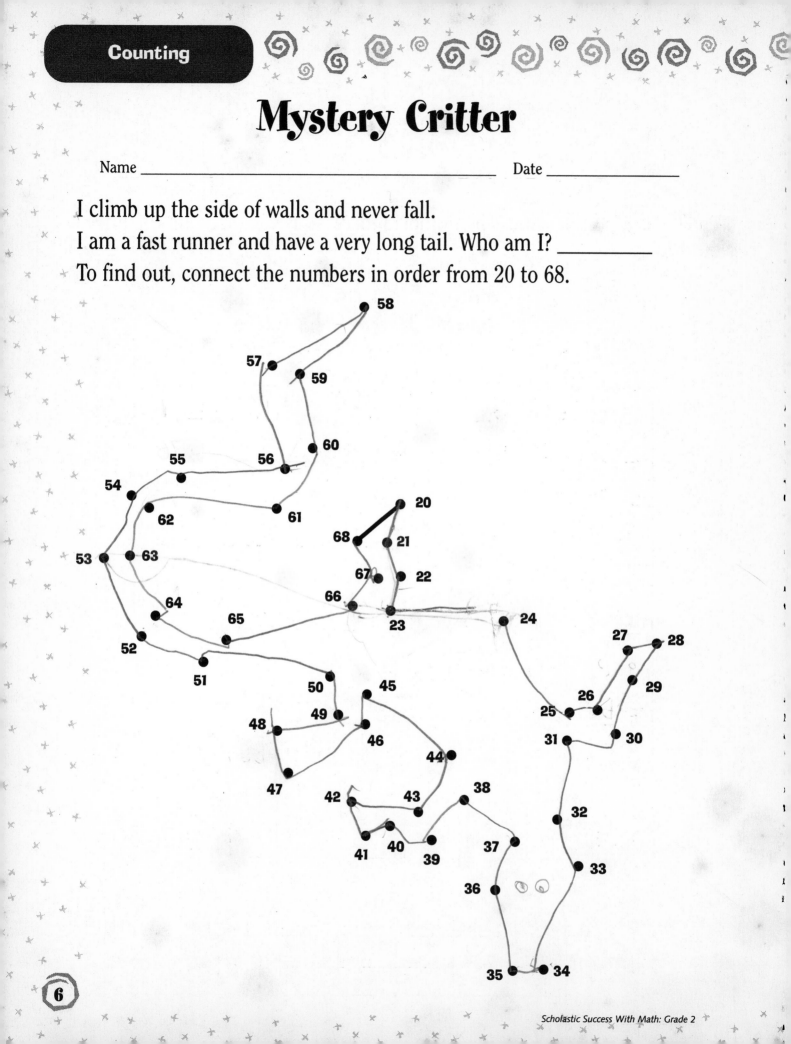

Patterns for the Mail Carrier

Name _____ Date _____

Meimei the mail carrier is delivering letters. Give her some help. Fill in the missing addresses on the houses below.

What pattern do you see in the house numbers? _____

_____

_____

_____

Presidents' Day Problem

Name _____ Date _____

The first 18 Presidents of the United States are listed below.
They are shown in order.

1. George Washington (1789–1797)
2. John Adams (1797–1801)
3. Thomas Jefferson (1801–1809)
4. James Madison (1809–1817)
5. James Monroe (1817–1825)
6. John Quincy Adams (1825–1829)
7. Andrew Jackson (1829–1837)
8. Martin Van Buren (1837–1841)
9. William Henry Harrison (1841)
10. John Tyler (1841–1845)
11. James Knox Polk (1845–1849)
12. Zachary Taylor (1849–1850)
13. Millard Fillmore (1850–1853)
14. Franklin Pierce (1853–1857)
15. James Buchanan (1857–1861)
16. Abraham Lincoln (1861–1865)
17. Andrew Johnson (1865–1869)
18. Ulysses S. Grant (1869–1877)

1. Which President was Washington? _____ **the 1st**

2. Which President was Lincoln? _____

3. Which President came before Lincoln? _____

4. Which President came after Lincoln? _____

5. How many Presidents were there
between Washington and Lincoln? _____

Pattern Learner

Name _____ Date _____

A pattern is a repeated arrangement of numbers, shapes, or lines in a row. Continue the patterns below.

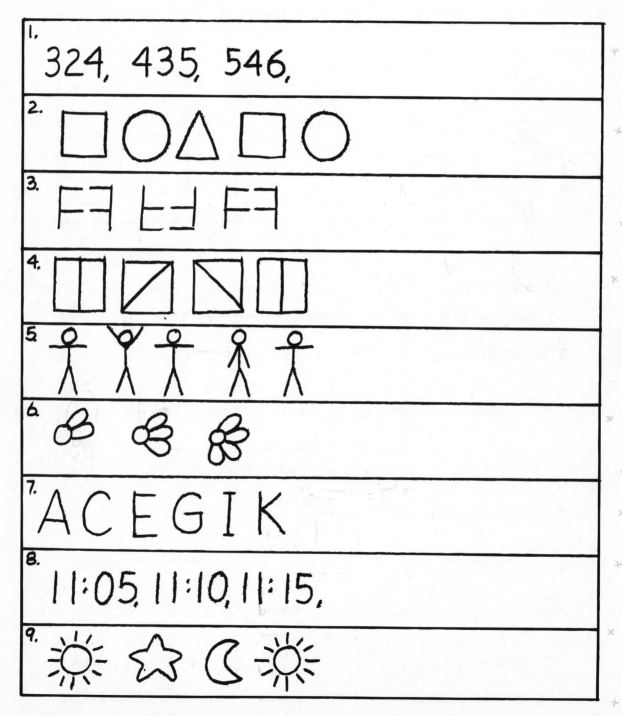

Shape Tricks

Name _____ Date _____

Danny's class was learning about shapes. He noticed that you could draw a line across one shape to make two shapes. Draw a line through each shape below to make two new shapes. (Pattern blocks may help you.)

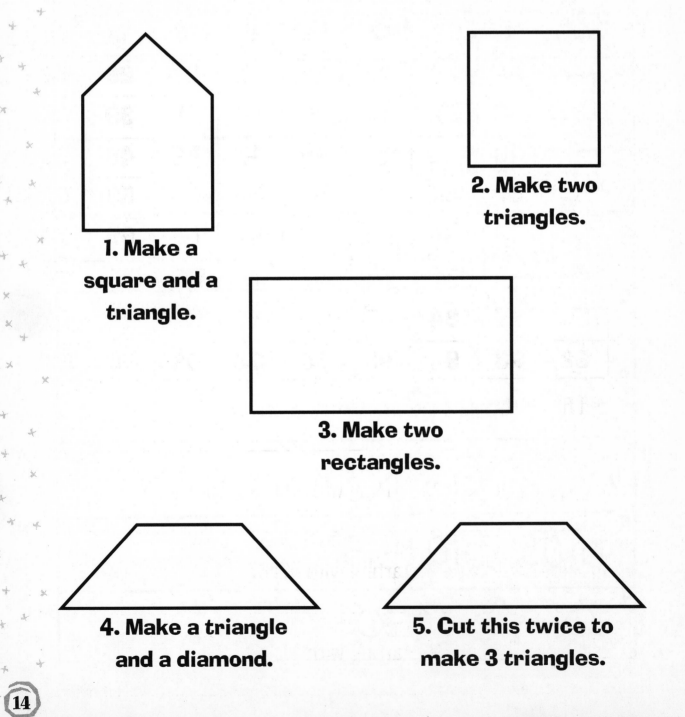

1. Make a square and a triangle.

2. Make two triangles.

3. Make two rectangles.

4. Make a triangle and a diamond.

5. Cut this twice to make 3 triangles.

14

Zoo Animal

Name _____ Date _____

1. Solve the problems.
2. Find each number pair on the graph. Make a dot for each.

3. Connect the dots in the order that you make them.
4. What picture did you make?

_____

	Across	Up
1.	13 + 7 = _____	12 + 4 = _____
2.	15 + 9 = _____	5 + 3 = _____
3.	11 + 9 = _____	0 + 4 = _____
4.	19 + 9 = _____	2 + 2 = _____
5.	10 + 18 = _____	11 + 5 = _____
6.	16 + 16 = _____	9 + 7 = _____
7.	28 + 8 = _____	2 + 6 = _____

	Across	Up
8.	17 + 15 = _____	1 + 3 = _____
9.	31 + 9 = _____	3 + 1 = _____
10.	8 + 32 = _____	8 + 8 = _____
11.	19 + 25 = _____	19 + 1 = _____
12.	27 + 17 = _____	18 + 14 = _____
13.	7 + 29 = _____	17 + 23 = _____
14.	18 + 6 = _____	25 + 15 = _____

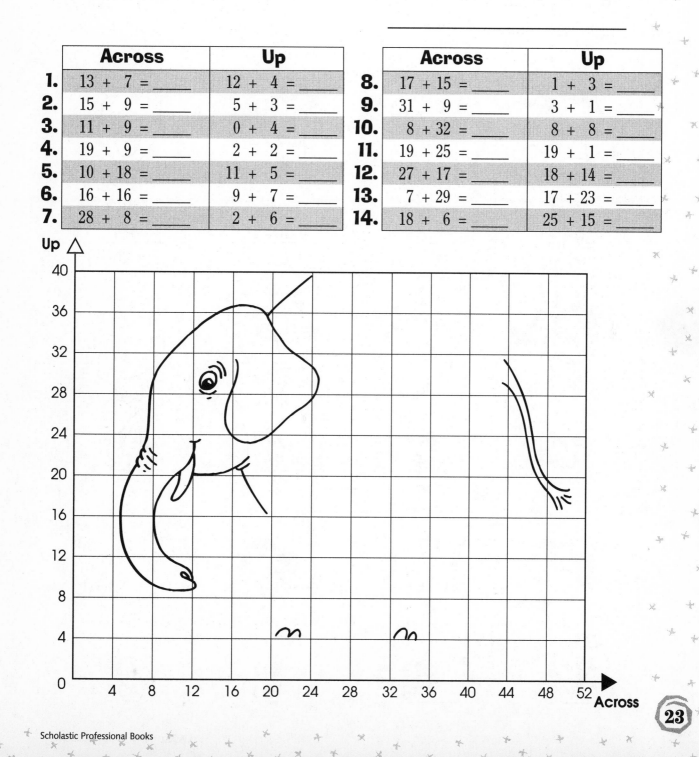

Tricky Twins

Name _____ Date _____

Sandy and Mandy are having a twin party. There are six sets of twins, but only one set of identical twins. To find the identical twins, solve the addition problems under each person. The identical twins have the same answer.

| 207 | 126 | 328 | 257 |
| + 544 | + 89 | + 348 | + 458 |

| 547 | 624 | 108 | 229 |
| + 129 | + 127 | + 107 | + 418 |

| 258 | 379 | 417 | 153 |
| + 268 | + 336 | + 109 | + 494 |

Time to Get Up!

Name _____ Date _____

Twenty animals were hibernating near Sleepy Pond.

5 of them woke up. Color 5 animals below.

How many are still sleeping? _____

A week later, 7 more woke up. Color 7 other animals.

How many are still sleeping? _____

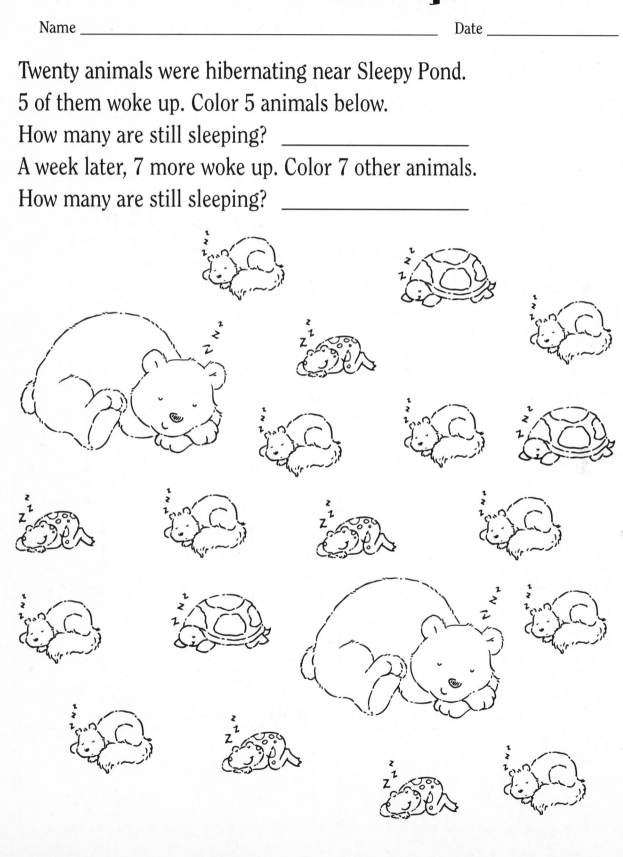

27

Detective Work

Name _____ Date _____

Use the code to help Detective Dave discover the secret phone number.
The first problem has been done for you.

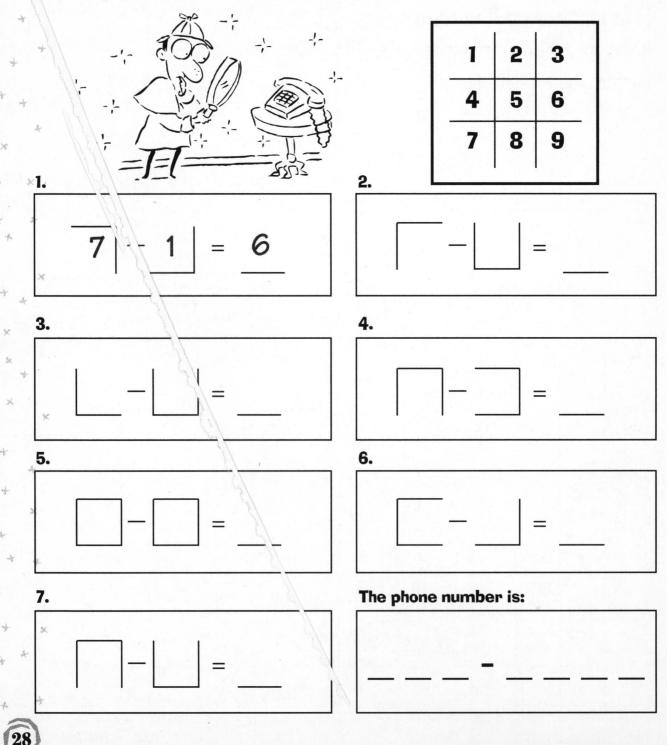

1	2	3
4	5	6
7	8	9

1.

$7 - 1 = 6$

2.

$\square - \square = \_\_$

3.

$\square - \square = \_\_$

4.

$\square - \square = \_\_$

5.

$\square - \square = \_\_$

6.

$\square - \square = \_\_$

7.

$\square - \square = \_\_$

The phone number is:

_ _ _ - _ _ _ _

Scholastic Success With Math: Grade 2

Chirp, Chirp!

Name _____ Date _____

1. Solve the problems.
2. Find each number pair on the graph. Make a dot for each.
3. Connect the dots in the order that you make them.
4. What picture did you make?

_____

	Across	Up
1.	10 – 7 = ____	10 – 8 = ____
2.	4 – 2 = ____	3 – 1 = ____
3.	7 – 5 = ____	1 – 0 = ____
4.	8 – 0 = ____	1 – 0 = ____
5.	9 – 1 = ____	8 – 6 = ____
6.	10 – 3 = ____	7 – 5 = ____
7.	10 – 2 = ____	8 – 2 = ____
8.	8 – 3 = ____	10 – 0 = ____
9.	9 – 7 = ____	7 – 1 = ____
10.	4 – 1 = ____	5 – 3 = ____
11.	9 – 2 = ____	6 – 4 = ____

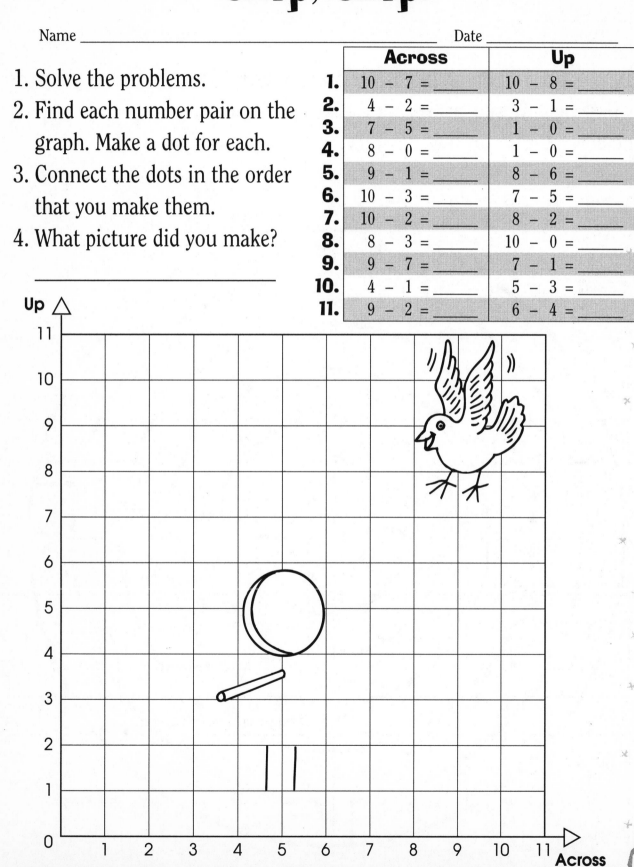

Winter Is Coming

Name _____ Date _____

Do the subtraction problems. Help Mr. Squirrel find his way to the tree where he is storing acorns for the winter. Make sure he doesn't cross any odd answers.

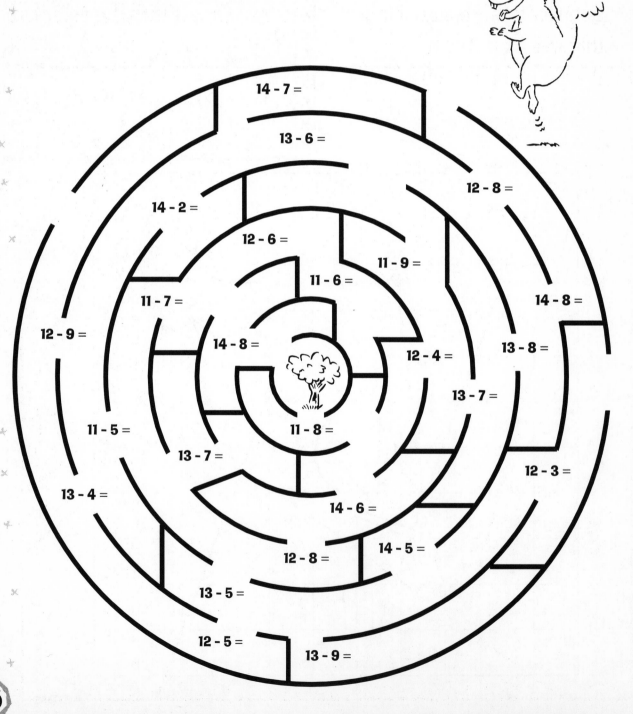

14 - 7 =

13 - 6 =

12 - 8 =

14 - 2 =

12 - 6 =

11 - 9 =

11 - 6 =

11 - 7 =

14 - 8 =

12 - 9 =

14 - 8 =

12 - 4 =

13 - 8 =

13 - 7 =

11 - 5 =

11 - 8 =

13 - 7 =

12 - 3 =

13 - 4 =

14 - 6 =

12 - 8 =

14 - 5 =

13 - 5 =

12 - 5 =

13 - 9 =

Baseball Puzzle

Name _____ Date _____

What animal can always be found at a baseball game?

_____

To find out, do the subtraction problems. If the answer is greater than 9, color the shapes black. If the answer is less than 10, color the shapes red.

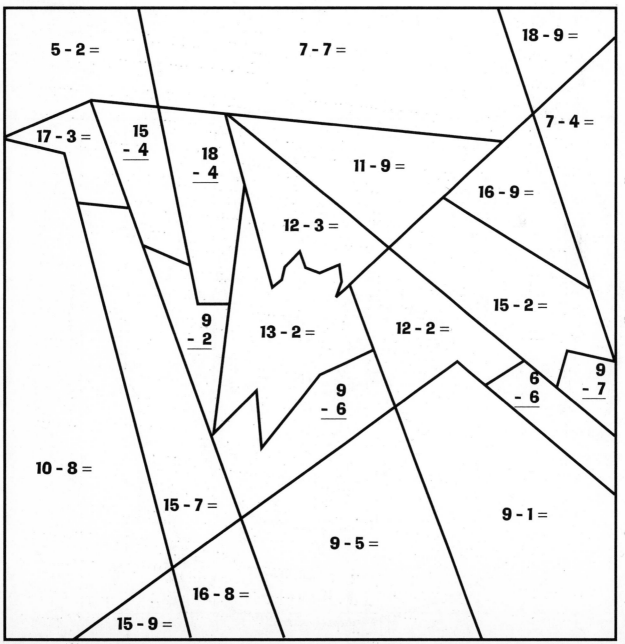

Bubble Yum!

Name _____ Date _____

1. Solve the problems.
2. Find each number pair on the graph. Make a dot for each.
3. Connect the dots in the order that you make them.
4. What picture did you make?

_____

	Across	Up
1.	27 – 23 = _____	58 – 53 = _____
2.	18 – 15 = _____	23 – 21 = _____
3.	30 – 27 = _____	29 – 28 = _____
4.	18 – 11 = _____	46 – 45 = _____
5.	58 – 51 = _____	17 – 15 = _____
6.	28 – 22 = _____	49 – 44 = _____
7.	19 – 15 = _____	77 – 72 = _____

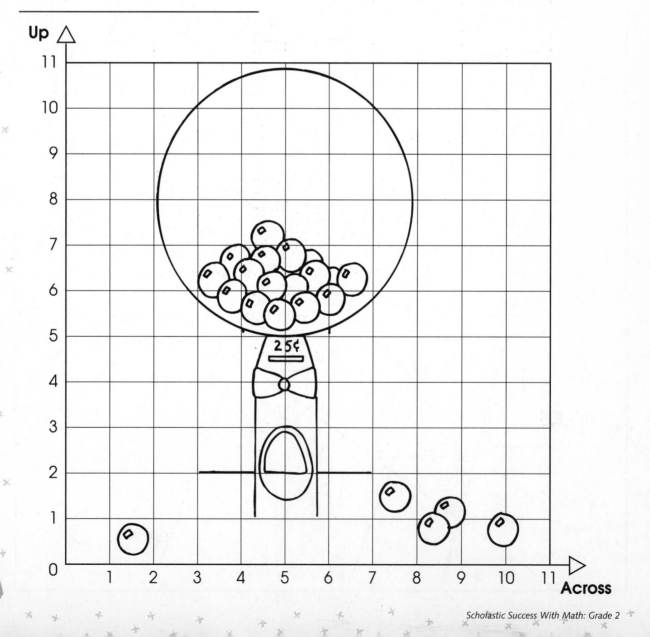

Super Star

Name _____ Date _____

Solve the problems. ✳ If the answer is between 1 and 20, color the shape red.
✳ If the answer is between 21 and 40, color the shape white. ✳ If the answer is
between 41 and 90, color the shape blue. ✳ *Taking It Further:* Write five
subtraction problems that have answers between 10 and 20.

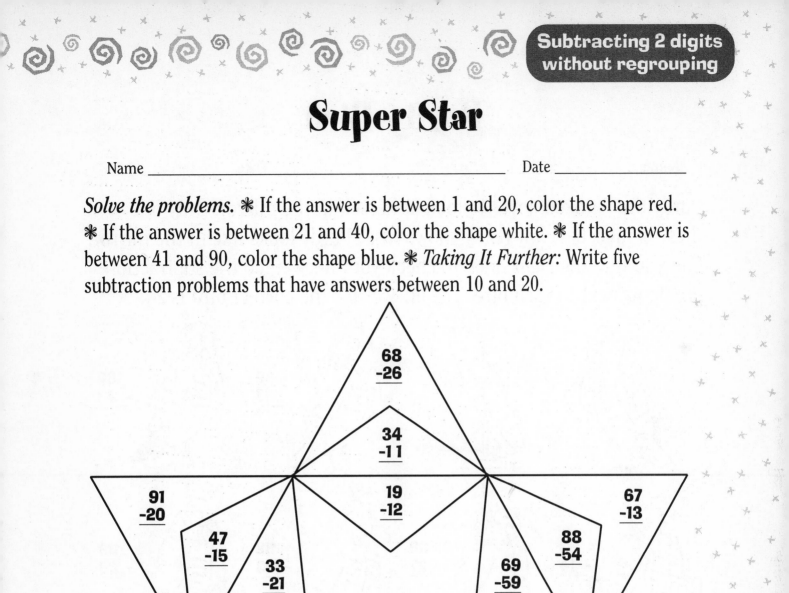

Purdy Bird

Name _____ Date _____

Purdy the Parakeet loves to look at herself in the mirror. Only one of these parakeets below really shows what Purdy looks like in the mirror. Can you find the right one? To check your answer, do the subtraction problems next to each bird. The answer for the correct bird is 24.

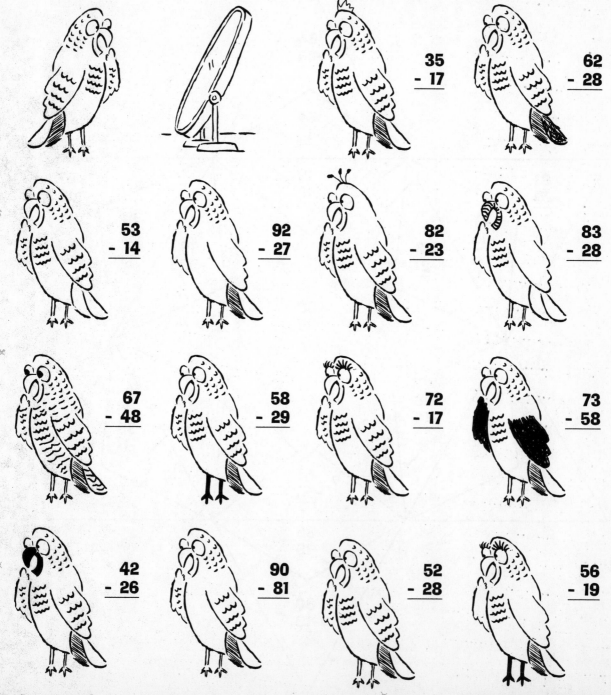

35 − 17

62 − 28

53 − 14

92 − 27

82 − 23

83 − 28

67 − 48

58 − 29

72 − 17

73 − 58

42 − 26

90 − 81

52 − 28

56 − 19

Grandma's Quilt

Name _____ Date _____

Solve the problems. ✳ If the answer is between 1 and 50, color the shape red.
✳ If the answer is between 51 and 100, color the shape blue. ✳ Finish the design
by coloring the other shapes with the colors of your choice. ✳ *Taking It Further:*
Amelia bought 30 tickets for rides at the carnival. She used 15 tickets in the
first hour. How many tickets did she have left?

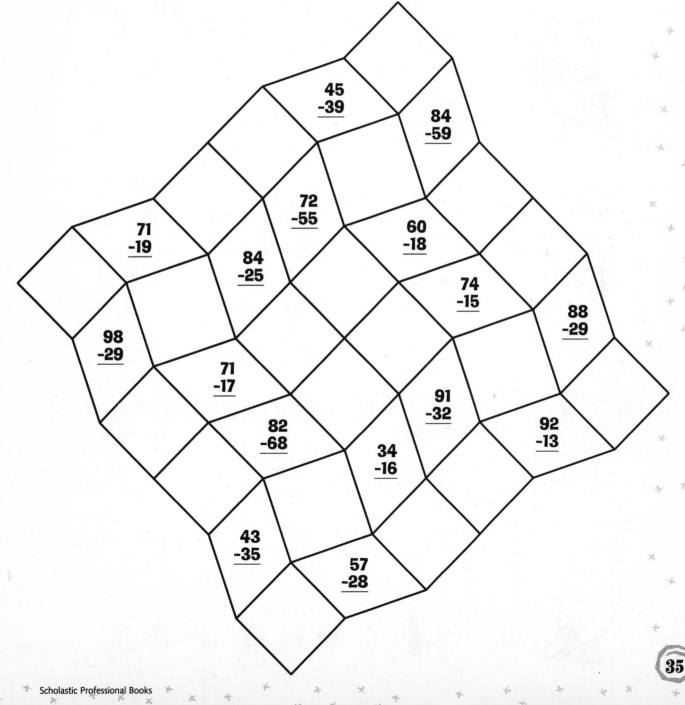

Rocket Riddle

Name _____ Date _____

What did the rocket say
when it left the party?

What To Do

To find the answer to the riddle,
solve the multiplication problems.
Then match each product with a
letter in the Key below. Write the
correct letters on the blanks below.

1   **5 x 1 =** _____   **6**   **5 x 2 =** _____

2   **8 x 1 =** _____   **7**   **6 x 2 =** _____

3   **11 x 1 =** _____   **8**   **8 x 2 =** _____

4   **26 x 1 =** _____   **9**   **9 x 2 =** _____

5   **3 x 2 =** _____   **10**   **12 x 2 =** _____

Key

10 . . . . F		27 . . . . U		20 . . . . W	
13 C		8 . . . . E		7 . . . . D	
11 . . . . O		6 . . . . K		12 . . . . T	
16 . . . . E		9 . . . . B		26 . . . . O	
5 . . . . A		24 . . . . F		18 . . . . T	

Riddle
Answer: "TIM __ __   __ __ __ __ __ __   __ __ __."
       8   **7** **3**   **9** **1** **5** **2**   **4** **6** **10**

Wise Owls

Name _____ Date _____

What did the owl say when someone knocked on its door?

What To Do

To find the answer to the riddle, solve the multiplication problems. Then match each product with a letter in the Key below. Write the correct letters on the blanks below.

1 5 x 3 = _____   **6** 6 x 3 = _____
2 2 x 3 = _____   **7** 10 x 3 = _____
3 8 x 3 = _____   **8** 12 x 3 = _____
4 4 x 3 = _____   **9** 11 x 3 = _____
5 9 x 3 = _____   **10** 0 x 3 = _____

Key

30 . . . . . . O	8 . . . . . . K	42 . . . . . . N
11 . . . . . . A	15 . . . . . . O	24 . . . . . . T
36 . . . . . . H	0 I	33 . . . . . . O
18 I	27 . . . . . . O	6 . . . . . . Q
32 . . . . . . F	6 . . . . . . S	12 . . . . . . W

Riddle Answer: " ___ ___ ___ ___ ___ ___ ___ ___ ___ ___ ?"
4 **8** **5** **9** **1** **7** **10** **2** **6** **3**

Jack's Beanstalk

Name _____ Date _____

Jack's class was growing bean plants. After 1 week, Jack's was the tallest.
Measure Jack's plant below. Record its height: _____
After 2 weeks, Jack's plant had doubled in height.
How tall was it now? _____

Draw a picture to show how tall the plant grew.
Measure your drawing to make sure it is the correct height.

2 weeks.

After 3 weeks, Jack's plant was still growing!
How tall would it be now? _____
Explain your answer. _____

_____

Candy Boxes

Name _____ Date _____

Steve works in a candy store. He puts candy into boxes. Each box has
10 spaces. Steve has 32 candies. Try to draw 32 candies in the boxes
below. Write the number of candies in each box on the line. Write the
number of any leftover candy at the bottom of the page.

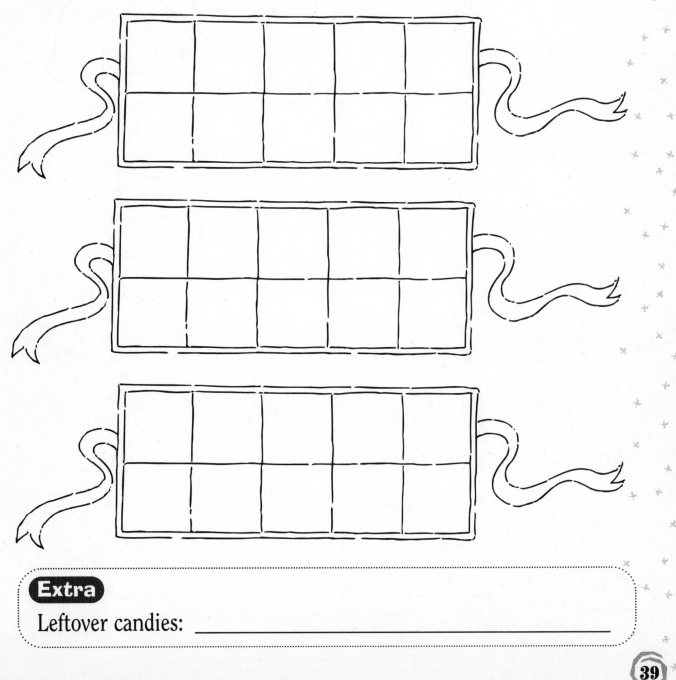

Extra

Leftover candies: _____

Creature Categories

Name _____ Date _____

Nick's class took a field trip to the beach. When they looked in the tide pools, they saw a lot of animals. Group the animals they saw. Color the animals in each group the same color.

Write a word or phrase that explains how you grouped them.

Group #1 _____

Group #2 _____

Group #3 _____

Coin-Toss Addition

Name _____ Date _____

Toss 8 coins. Write "H" for heads or "T" for tails in the circles below to show your toss. Then write the addition equation. Write the number of "heads" first. We did the first one for you. Try it three times.

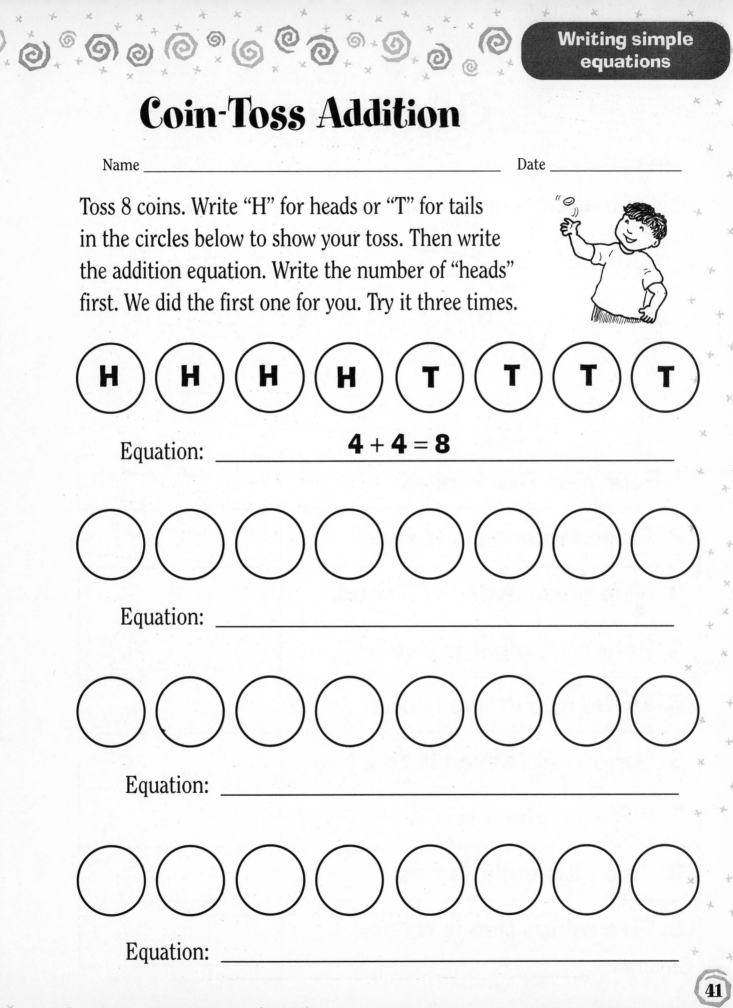

(H) (H) (H) (H) (T) (T) (T) (T)

Equation: _____ 4 + 4 = 8 _____

◯ ◯ ◯ ◯ ◯ ◯ ◯ ◯

Equation: _____

◯ ◯ ◯ ◯ ◯ ◯ ◯ ◯

Equation: _____

◯ ◯ ◯ ◯ ◯ ◯ ◯ ◯

Equation: _____

Clear Reader

Name _____ Date _____

Write each sentence using numbers and symbols.

1. Four plus five is nine.	
2. Eleven minus six is five.	
3. Nine plus seven is sixteen.	
4. Four plus eight is twelve.	
5. Three minus two is one.	
6. Seven plus seven is fourteen.	
7. Fifteen minus ten is five.	
8. Two plus eight is ten.	
9. Five minus two is three.	

Scholastic Success With Math: Grade 2

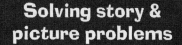
Flower Problems

Name _____ Date _____

Solve these story problems. Cut out the flowers at the bottom of the
page to help you.

1. Jared had a flowerpot with 7 flowers.
   He replanted 5 flowers outdoors. How
   many flowers were left in the pot?

   _____

2. Kristin planted 7 flowers.
   1 flower wilted. How many flowers were not wilted?

   _____

3. Hannah picked flowers for her father.
   She picked 3 flowers from the front yard.
   She picked 4 flowers from the back yard.
   She put them in a flowerpot.
   How many flowers did Hannah pick?

   _____

Pizza Party

Name _____ Date _____

Garth's class is having a pizza party. They made a diagram to show which pizzas they would like. Draw an X in each circle to show how many classmates wanted each kind of pizza.

- 5 wanted cheese pizza.
- 10 wanted pepperoni pizza.
- 3 wanted sausage pizza.
- 2 wanted both cheese and pepperoni pizza.

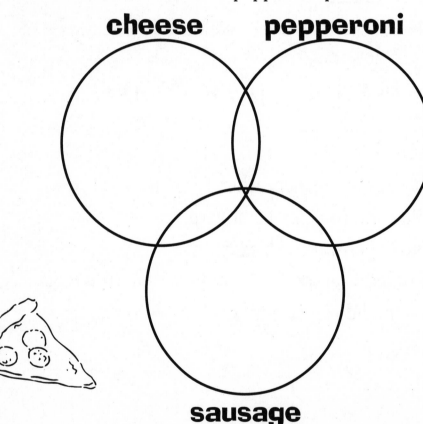

What can you learn by looking at this diagram? Write your ideas:

_____

_____

Prime Timer

Name _____ Date _____

WRITE THE TIME 3 WAYS.

example: 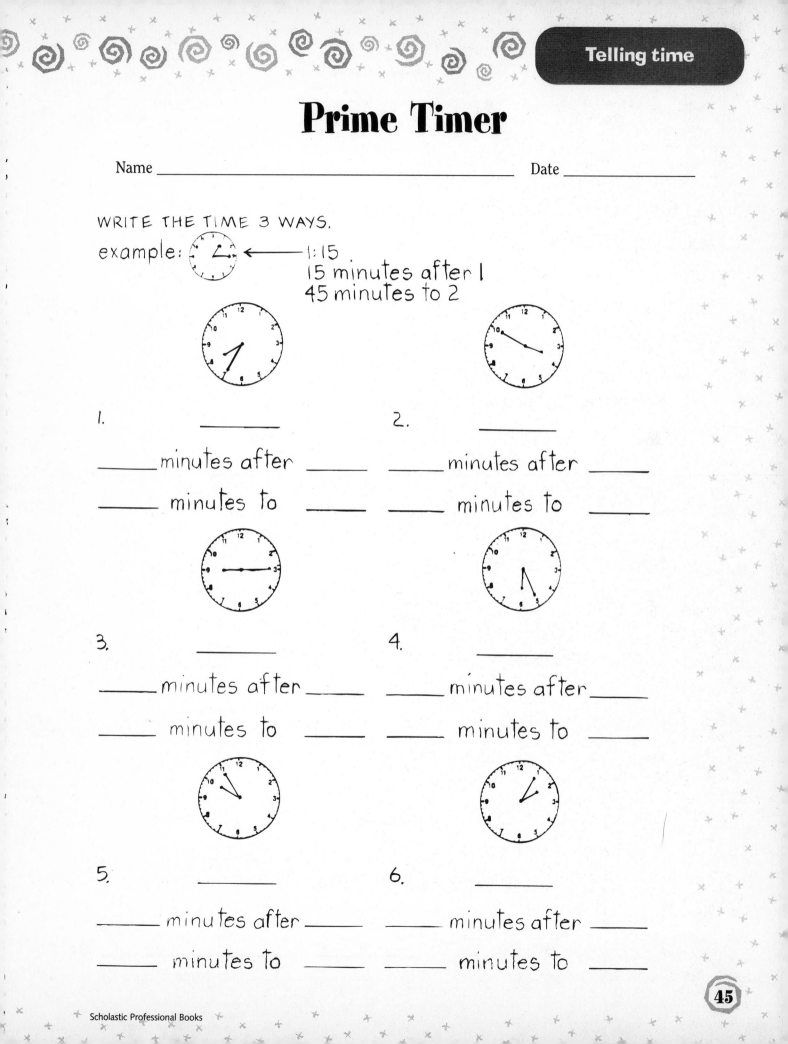 ←———— 1:15
15 minutes after 1
45 minutes to 2

1. _____

_____ minutes after _____

_____ minutes to _____

2. _____

_____ minutes after _____

_____ minutes to _____

3. _____

_____ minutes after _____

_____ minutes to _____

4. _____

_____ minutes after _____

_____ minutes to _____

5. _____

_____ minutes after _____

_____ minutes to _____

6. _____

_____ minutes after _____

_____ minutes to _____

Just Snacks

Name _____ Date _____

Use the menu on page 47 to answer the following questions.

1. Which snack costs the most?

    _____

    How much do they cost?

    _____

2. Which sweet costs the least? _____

    How much does it cost?   _____

3. Henry spends 50¢ on a snack.
    What does he buy? _____

4. Gina orders a drink. She spends 15¢.
    Which drink does she order?   _____

5. Dan orders popcorn and a cookie.
    How much does he pay?   _____

6. Pat buys a cup of soup and a sip of milk.
    How much does she spend? _____

Small Snacks

Potato Chips .... 60¢

Pretzels .... 45¢

Popcorn .... 55¢

Peanuts .... 50¢

Bagel Bites .... 65¢

Teeny Sandwiches .... 75¢

Cup of Soup .... 40¢

Small Sweets & Drinks

Cookie .... 40¢

Donut Hole .... 25¢

Ice Cream Bar .... 60¢

Raisins .... 30¢

Sip of Milk .... 10¢

Gulp of Juice .... 15¢

47

Money Matters

Name_____ Date _____

Alex asked his little brother Billy to trade piggy banks.

Alex's bank has these coins: Billy's has these coins:

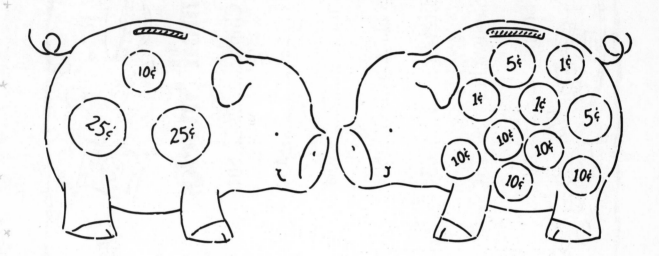

Do you think this is a fair trade? _____

Test your answer:

Add up Alex's coins: _____

Add up Billy's coins: _____

Write the totals in this Greater Than/Less Than equation:

_____ > _____

Who has more money? _____

Best Estimator

Name_____ Date _____

LENGTH CAN BE MEASURED IN INCHES (IN.), FEET (FT.), YARDS (YD.), AND MILES (MI.). 12 IN. = 1 FT. 5280 FT. = 1 MILE.

UNDERLINE THE MORE SENSIBLE MEASURE.

How many inches to Boston, Sir?

BUS STOP

1. HEIGHT OF A BOOKCASE
   INCHES   FEET

2. WIDTH OF YOUR BACKYARD
   YARDS   MILES

3. LENGTH OF A RIVER
   MILES   YARDS

4. WIDTH OF A DESK
   INCHES   FEET

5. LENGTH OF YOUR ARM
   FEET   INCHES

6. LENGTH OF A COMB
   INCHES   FEET

7. LENGTH OF A FOOTBALL FIELD
   INCHES   YARDS

8. DISTANCE FROM EARTH TO MOON
   MILES   YARDS

9. DEPTH OF A SWIMMING POOL
   FEET   INCHES

10. TUBE OF TOOTHPASTE
    INCHES   FEET

11. HEIGHT OF A REFRIGERATOR
    INCHES   FEET

12. WIDTH OF A BEDROOM
    FEET   INCHES

13. DISTANCE BETWEEN 2 CITIES
    YARDS   MILES

14. LENGTH OF A DOLLAR
    INCHES   FEET

15. LENGTH OF AN AUTOMOBILE
    INCHES   FEET

Zoo Weigh-In

Name _____ Date _____

Zoey's class went to the zoo. They wrote down how much the animals weighed. Cut out the animals below. Arrange them in weight order—from lightest to heaviest.

329 lbs

358 lbs.

224 lbs.

532 lbs.

Measuring Perimeter

Name _____ Date _____

Use the inch side of a ruler and measure each side of each triangle. Write the inches in the spaces below. Then add up all the sides to find the perimeter, or distance around each triangle.

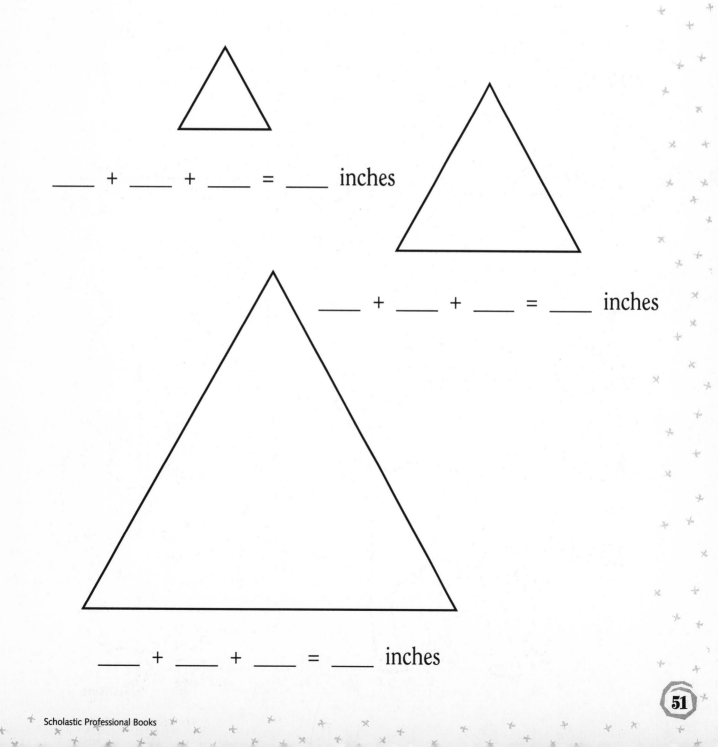

___ + ___ + ___ = ___ inches

___ + ___ + ___ = ___ inches

___ + ___ + ___ = ___ inches

Scholastic Professional Books

Night-Light

Name _____ Date _____

1. Find each number pair on the graph. Make a dot for each.
2. Connect the dots in the order that you make them.
3. What picture did you make?

   _____

	Across	Up
1.	6	11
2.	5	7
3.	1	7
4.	4	5
5.	3	0
6.	6	3
7.	9	0
8.	8	5
9.	11	7
10.	7	7
11.	6	11

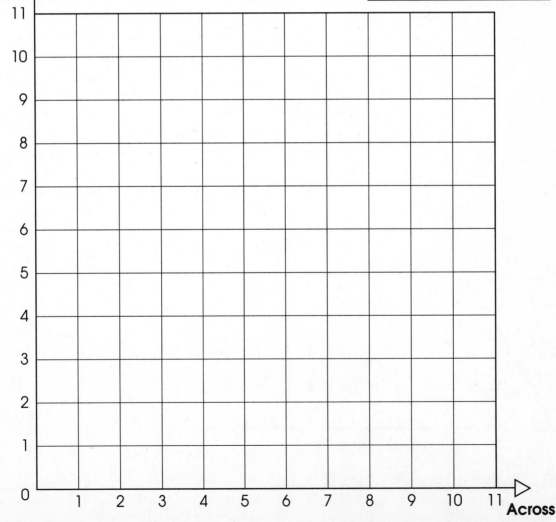

Great Graphing

Name _____ Date _____

The picture was made with 7 different shapes. How many of each shape
was used? Color in the shapes, following the instructions. Then color in
the boxes on the chart, 1 box for each shape used.

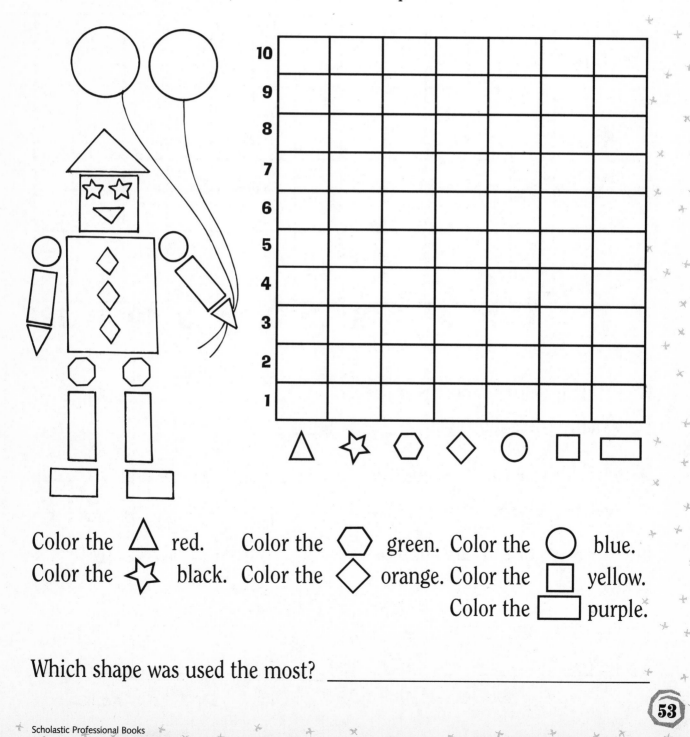

Color the △ red. Color the ⬡ green. Color the ○ blue.
Color the ☆ black. Color the ◇ orange. Color the ☐ yellow.
                                       Color the ▭ purple.

Which shape was used the most? _____

53

Fruit Graph

Name _____ Date _____

Ask 12 friends which of these four fruits they like most. Fill in the graph to find out. Color one box on the graph for each vote.

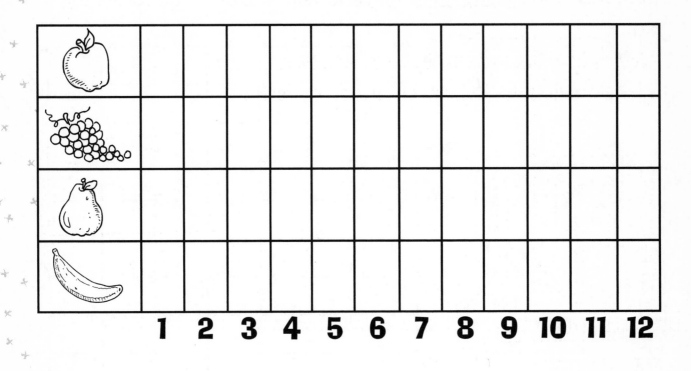

Which fruit was the most popular?   _____

How many votes did it get?   _____

Which fruit was the least popular?   _____

How many votes did it get?   _____

If two fruits got the same amount of votes, they "tied." Write any ties below.

_____ and _____

_____ and _____

Chester's Cakes and Pies

Name _____ Date _____

Fill in the blanks. Chester Chipmunk was cutting cakes and pies.
Bobby Bear said, "Some aren't cut in half. When you cut something in
half, there are _____ pieces and both of the pieces are the
same _____."
Here is how Chester cut the cakes and pies.
Circle the desserts that are cut in half correctly.

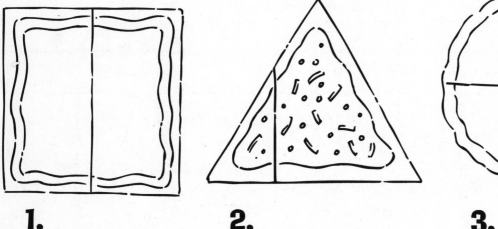

1.   **2.**   **3.**

4.

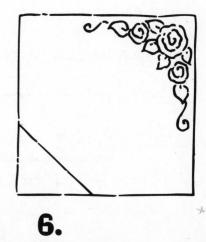

5.   **6.**

Part Timer

Name _____ Date _____

Determine fractions of a whole. Check √ your answers.

1. HOW MUCH JUICE IS LEFT?

$\frac{1}{2}$
$\frac{1}{4}$
$\frac{1}{3}$

2. HOW MUCH PIZZA IS GONE?

$\frac{1}{2}$
$\frac{1}{3}$
$\frac{1}{8}$

3. HOW MUCH HAS BEEN EATEN?

$\frac{1}{3}$
$\frac{1}{6}$
$\frac{1}{4}$

4. HOW MUCH IS GONE?

$\frac{1}{4}$
$\frac{1}{2}$
$\frac{1}{8}$

5. HOW MUCH IS LACED?

$\frac{1}{2}$
$\frac{1}{3}$
$\frac{1}{4}$

6. HOW MUCH TONIC IS LEFT?

$\frac{1}{6}$
$\frac{1}{4}$
$\frac{1}{3}$

7. HOW MUCH WATER IS LEFT?

$\frac{3}{4}$
$\frac{1}{2}$
$\frac{1}{4}$

8. HOW MUCH HAS BEEN CUT OFF?

$\frac{1}{2}$
$\frac{1}{3}$
$\frac{1}{4}$

9. HOW MUCH WATER REMAINS?

$\frac{3}{4}$ $\frac{1}{2}$ $\frac{1}{4}$

10. HOW MUCH LEAF HAS BEEN EATEN?

$\frac{1}{4}$
$\frac{1}{6}$
$\frac{2}{3}$

11. HOW MUCH BREAD IS UNCUT?

$\frac{1}{4}$ $\frac{1}{3}$ $\frac{1}{2}$

56

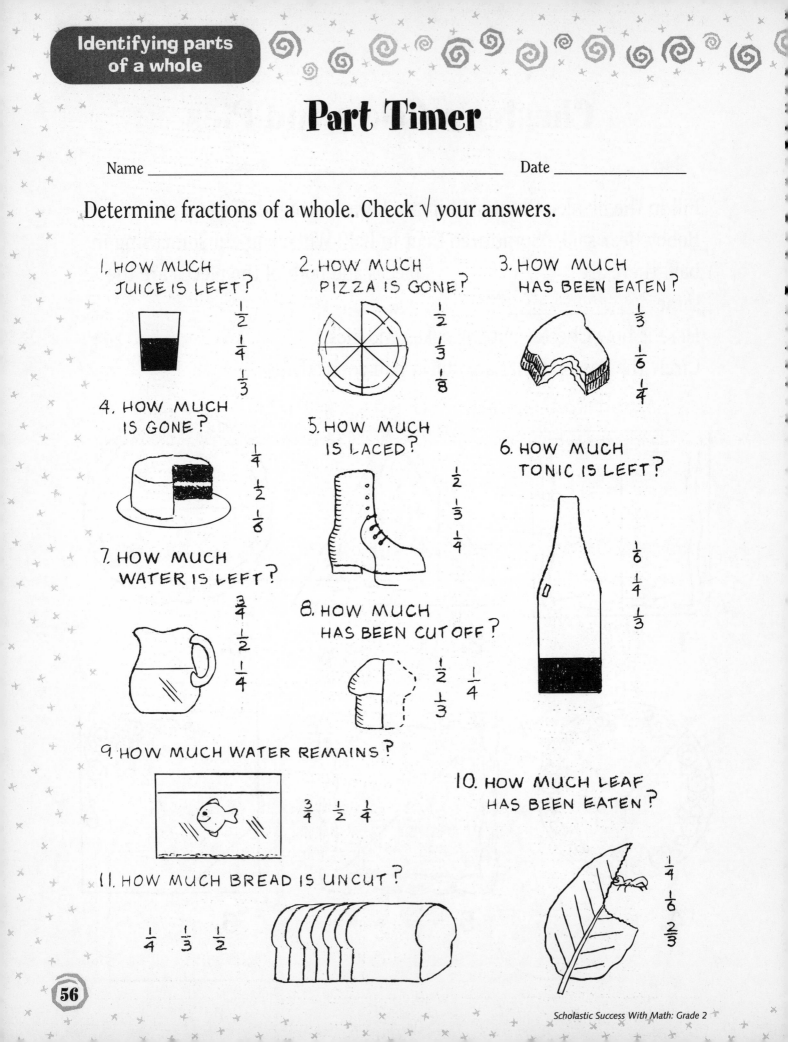

Fraction Fun

Name _____ Date _____

Something that is split in 2 equal parts is divided in "half."

These two shapes are divided in half.

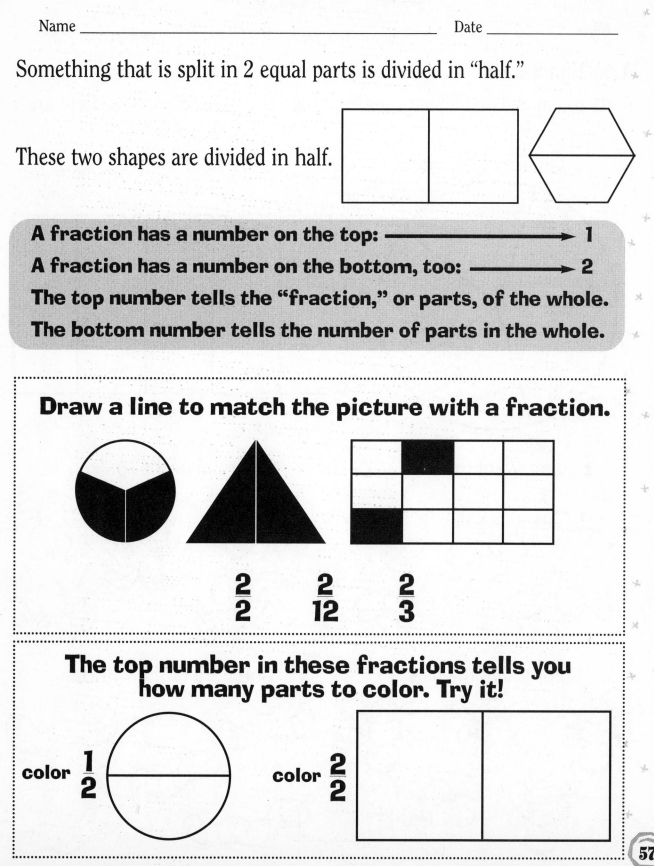

A fraction has a number on the top: ——————→ **1**

A fraction has a number on the bottom, too: ——————→ **2**

The top number tells the "fraction," or parts, of the whole.

The bottom number tells the number of parts in the whole.

Draw a line to match the picture with a fraction.

$\dfrac{2}{2}$ $\dfrac{2}{12}$ $\dfrac{2}{3}$

The top number in these fractions tells you how many parts to color. Try it!

color $\dfrac{1}{2}$ color $\dfrac{2}{2}$

57

Fun With Fractions

Name_____ Date _____

A fraction has two numbers. The top number will tell you how many parts to color. The bottom number tells you how many parts there are.

Color 1/5 of the circle.

Color 4/5 of the rectangle.

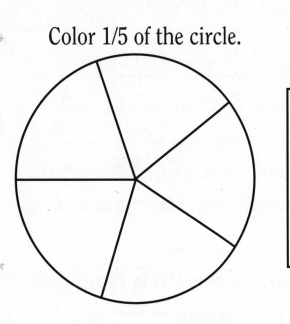

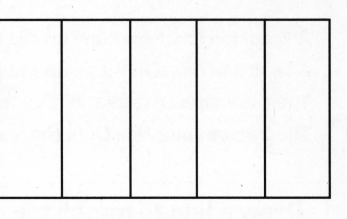

Color 3/5 of the ants.

Color 2/5 of the spiders.

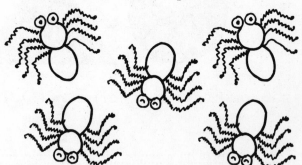

Color 0/5 of the bees.

Color 5/5 of the worms.

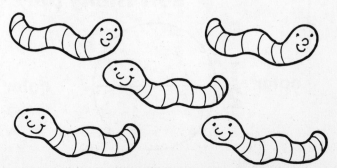

58

Scholastic Success With Math: Grade 2

More Fun With Fractions

Name _____ Date _____

A fraction has two numbers. The top number will tell you how many parts to color. The bottom number tells you how many total parts there are.

$\frac{10}{10}$ is the whole circle.

Color $\frac{8}{10}$ of the circle.

How much is not colored? ____

$\frac{10}{10}$ is the whole rectangle.

Color $\frac{4}{10}$ of the rectangle.

How much is not colored? ____

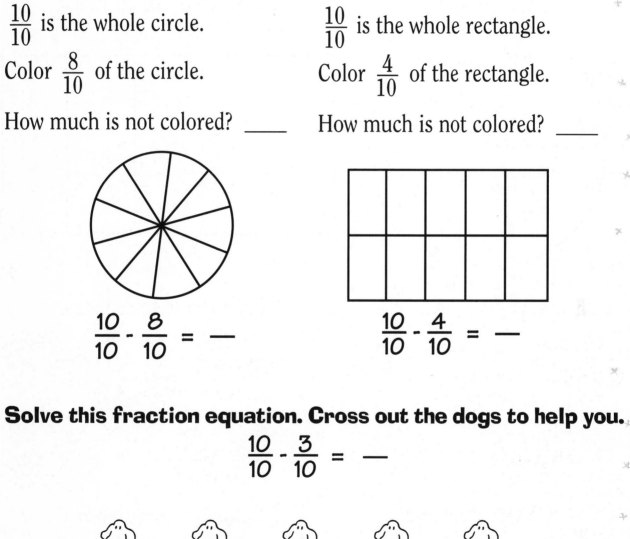

$$\frac{10}{10} - \frac{8}{10} = \underline{}$$

$$\frac{10}{10} - \frac{4}{10} = \underline{}$$

Solve this fraction equation. Cross out the dogs to help you.

$$\frac{10}{10} - \frac{3}{10} = \underline{}$$

Answer Key

Page 5

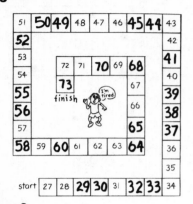

Page 6

A salamander

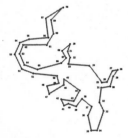

Page 7

1. 67; **2.** 34, 35; **3.** 42, 43; **4.** 16, 18
5. 73, 74, 75; **6.** 31, 32; **7.** 10 12 14 16
8. 15 18 21 24; **9.** 83, 84, 85, 86, 87, 88
10. after; **11.** before; **12.** after
13. before; **14.** before; **15.** before

Page 8

Students should follow these numbers:
13, 7, 3, 9, 19, 23, 11, 5, 17, 67, 33, 25,
27, 35, 39, 37, 23, 57, 47, 43, 21, 15, 39, 29

Page 9

Top side of the street: 50, 52, 54, 56
Bottom side of the street: 51, 53, 55
Extra: The even numbers are on one side of the street.
The odd numbers are on the other side of the street.

Page 10

1. the 1st **2.** the 16th **3.** James Buchanan
4. Andrew Johnson **5.** 14

Page 11

1. 11 < 21; **2.** 56 < 72; **3.** 47 = 47; **4.** 64 >10
5. 59 = 59; **6.** 38 >17; **7.** 526 < 527; **8.** 159 > 42
9–16. Answers will vary. **17.** 73 61 54 37
18. 96 43 24 22; **19.** 79 78 69 51
20. 51 37 27 15

Page 12

A sidewalk.
518, 315, 276, 693, 137, 564, 909, 811, 209, 717, 836, 321,
488, 857, 432, 707

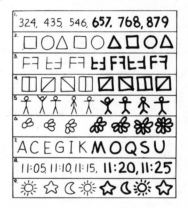

Page 13

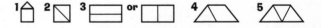

Page 14

This line   This line
could move   could move
up or down.   left or right.

Page 15

1. 32, 42, 52, 62, 72, 82, 92
2. 70, 60, 50, 40, 30, 20, 10
3. 67, 57, 47, 37, 27, 17, 7
4. 44, 55, 66, 77, 88, 99

Page 16

Answers will vary.

Page 17

A. 1F, 2G, 3B, 4C **or** A, 5E, 6I, 7E, 8H, 9G, 10G, 11C
B. 1B, 2F, 3D, 4I, 5F, 6E, 7A, 8D, 9I, 10F, 11I
C. 1H, 2C, 3C, 4G, 5G, 6C, 7F, 8I, 9B, 10C **or** A, 11F

Page 18

Beans talk
4 + 2 = 6; 7 + 7 = 14; 9 + 5 = 14; 10 + 4 = 14;
4 + 8 = 12; 6 + 8 = 14; 11 + 3 = 14; 14 + 0 = 14;
7 + 2 = 9; 13 + 1 = 14; 5 + 8 = 13; 12 + 2 = 14;
7 + 4 = 11; 5 + 9 = 14

Page 19

1. 21; 2. 26; 3. 14; 4. 31
5. 35; 6. 28; 7. 27; 8. 29
9. 58; 10. 33

Page 20

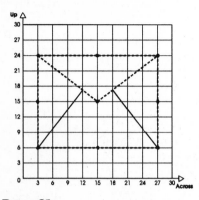

Page 21

2 + 8 = 10; 24 + 7 = 31; 32 + 9 = 41; 1 + 9 = 10;
7 + 4 = 11; 45 + 5 = 50; 31 + 4 = 35; 11 + 9 = 20;
17 + 9 = 26; 22 + 13 = 35; 26 + 6 = 32; 19 + 9 = 28;
11 + 7 = 18; 16 + 22 = 38; 31 + 11 = 42; 14 + 9 = 23;
12 + 7 = 19; 40 + 14 = 54; 27 + 6 = 33; 12 + 9 = 21;
4 + 8 = 12; 41 + 21 = 62; 37 + 31 = 68; 16 + 6 = 22;
16 + 5 = 21; 10 + 24 = 34; 20 + 21 = 41; 15 + 5 = 20

Extra: Answers will vary.

Page 22

15 + 33 + 27 = 75; 27 + 23 + 12 = 62;
34 + 23 + 24 = 81; 15 + 25 + 10 = 50;
16 + 14 + 14 = 44; 12 + 31 + 17 = 60;
28 + 22 + 45 = 95; 43 + 27 + 27 = 97;
10 + 17 + 18 = 45; 29 + 13 + 16 = 58;
37 + 31 + 17 = 85; 51 + 23 + 17 = 91

Page 23

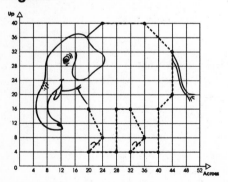

Page 24

207 + 544 = 751; 126 + 89 = 215;
328 + 348 = 676; 257 + 458 = 715;
547 + 129 = 676; 624 + 127 = 751;
108 + 107 = 215; 229 + 418 = 647;
258 + 268 = 526; 379 + 336 = 715;
417 + 109 = 526; 153 + 494 = 647

Page 25

Page 26

1. 9R1; 2. 3R3; 3. 4R0; 4. 5R0; 5. 2R0
6. 6R1; 7. 3R0; 8. 9R2; 9. 6R0; 10. 4R3

Page 27

15; 8

Page 28

1. 7 − 1 = 6; 2. 9 − 2 = 7; 3. 3 − 2 = 1; 4. 8 − 4 = 4
5. 5 − 5 = 0; 6. 6 − 1 = 5; 7. 8 − 2 = 6
The phone number is 671-4056.

Page 29

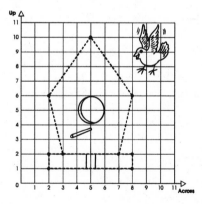

Page 30

Page 31

A bat

$5 - 2 = 3$; $7 - 7 = 0$; $18 - 9 = 9$; $17 - 3 = 14$; $15 - 4 = 11$
$18 - 4 = 14$; $12 - 3 = 9$; $11 - 9 = 2$; $16 - 9 = 7$; $7 - 4 = 3$
$10 - 8 = 2$; $15 - 7 = 8$; $9 - 2 = 7$; $13 - 2 = 11$; $12 - 2 = 10$
$15 - 2 = 13$; $9 - 6 = 3$; $6 - 6 = 0$; $9 - 7 = 2$; $15 - 9 = 6$
$16 - 8 = 8$; $9 - 5 = 4$; $9 - 1 = 8$

Page 32

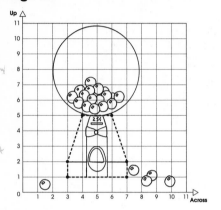

Page 33

$68 - 26 = 42$; $34 - 11 = 23$; $91 - 20 = 71$
$47 - 15 = 32$; $67 - 13 = 54$; $88 - 54 = 34$
$19 - 12 = 7$; $33 - 21 = 12$; $69 - 59 = 10$
$88 - 12 = 76$; $28 - 24 = 4$; $17 - 6 = 11$
$57 - 55 = 2$; $27 - 5 = 22$; $97 - 13 = 84$
$35 - 11 = 24$; $81 - 21 = 60$; $39 - 15 = 24$
$60 - 10 = 50$

Page 34

$35 - 17 = 18$; $62 - 28 = 34$; $53 - 14 = 39$; $92 - 27 = 65$
$82 - 23 = 59$; $83 - 28 = 55$; $67 - 48 = 19$; $58 - 29 = 29$
$72 - 17 = 55$; $73 - 58 = 15$; $42 - 26 = 16$; $90 - 81 = 9$
$52 - 28 = 24$; $56 - 19 = 37$

Page 35

$45 - 39 = 6$; $84 - 59 = 25$; $72 - 55 = 17$
$71 - 19 = 52$; $84 - 25 = 59$; $60 - 18 = 42$
$98 - 29 = 69$; $74 - 15 = 59$; $71 - 17 = 54$
$88 - 29 = 59$; $82 - 68 = 14$; $91 - 32 = 59$
$34 - 16 = 18$; $92 - 13 = 79$; $43 - 35 = 8$; $57 - 28 = 29$
She had 15 tickets left.

Page 36

1. 5; **2.** 8; **3.** 11; **4.** 26; **5.** 6
6. 10; **7.** 12; **8.** 16; **9.** 18; **10.** 24
What did the rocket say when it left the party?
"Time to take off."

Page 37

1. 15; **2.** 6; **3.** 24; **4.** 12; **5.** 27
6. 18; **7.** 30; **8.** 36; **9.** 33; **10.** 0
What did the owl say when someone knocked on its door?
"Whoooo is it?"

Page 38

2 inches; 4 inches
Two possible answers:
  6 inches, because it grew 2 inches each week;
  or 8 inches, because it doubled in height each week

Page 39

10, 10, 10 **Extra:** 2

Page 40

3 groups: fish, shells, animals with multiple legs/arms

Page 41

Answers will vary.

Page 42

1. $4 + 5 = 9$; **2.** $11 - 6 = 5$; **3.** $9 + 7 = 16$
4. $4 + 8 = 12$; **5.** $3 - 2 = 1$; **6.** $7 + 7 = 14$
7. $15 - 10 = 5$; **8.** $2 + 8 = 10$; **9.** $5 - 2 = 3$

Page 43

1. 2; **2.** 6; **3.** 7

Page 44

Extra: Answers will vary. Possible: Pepperoni is the most popular topping. Cheese is the next favorite topping. Sausage is the least favorite topping.

Page 45

1. 7:35, 35 minutes after 7, 25 minutes to 8
2. 3:50, 50 minutes after 3, 10 minutes to 4
3. 9:15, 15 minutes after 9, 45 minutes to 10
4. 6:25, 25 minutes after 6, 35 minutes to 7
5. 9:55, 55 minutes after 9, 5 minutes to 10
6. 2:05, 5 minutes after 2, 55 minutes to 3

Pages 46-47

1. Teeny Sandwiches; 75¢
2. Donut Hole; 25¢
3. Peanuts
4. Gulp of Juice
5. 95¢ **6.** 50¢

Page 48

Alex's coins: $5¢ + 25¢ + 10¢ = 60¢$
Billy's coins: $10¢ + 10¢ + 10¢ + 10¢ + 10¢ + 5¢ + 5¢ + 1¢ +$
                $1¢ + 1¢ = 63¢$
$63¢ > 60¢$ Billy has more money.

Page 49

1. feet; **2.** yards; **3.** miles; **4.** inches; **5.** inches
6. inches; **7.** yards; **8.** miles; **9.** feet; **10.** inches
11. feet; **12.** feet; **13.** miles; **14.** inches; **15.** feet

Page 50

deer (224 pounds), seal (329 pounds),
lion (358 pounds), bear (532 pounds)

Page 51

$1 + 1 + 1 = 3$ inches
$2 + 2 + 2 = 6$ inches
$4 + 4 + 4 = 12$ inches

Page 52

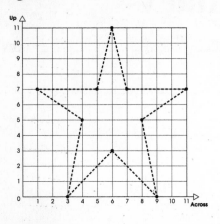

Page 53

the rectangle

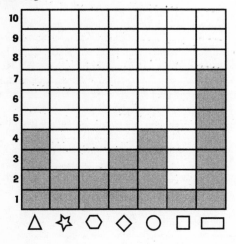

Page 54

Answers will vary.

Page 55

2, size; Correct pies: 1, 3, 5

Page 56

1. 1/2; **2.** 1/8; **3.** 1/4; **4.** 1/4; **5.** 1/2; **6.** 1/6
7. 1/2; **8.** 1/2; **9.** 3/4; **10.** 1/4; **11.** 1/2

Page 57

2/2 matches triangle, 2/3 matches circle,
2/12 matches rectangle; color 1/2 circle,
color the whole rectangle

Page 58

1/5 of the circle, 4/5 of the rectangle,
3 ants, 2 spiders, 0 bees, 5 worms

Page 59

2/10, 6/10, 2/10, 6/10, 7/10

Instant Skills Index

SECTION AND SKILL ....*PAGES*

NUMBER CONCEPTS
    Missing numbers 5, 7
    Counting 5, 6, 7
    Odd and even numbers 8, 9, 30
    Ordinal numbers 10
    Greater than, less than, equal to 11
    Place value 12

SHAPES AND PATTERNS
    Identifying patterns 13, 15
    Identifying shapes 14, 16, 17
    Combining shapes 14, 53
    Three-dimensional shapes 17

ADDITION
    Adding 1 and 2 digits without regrouping 18, 20, 41
    Column addition 19, 22
    Adding 1 and 2 digits with regrouping 21, 23
    Adding 2 and 3 digits with regrouping 22, 24, 25
    Missing addends 25

SUBTRACTION
    Related addition and subtraction 26, 27
    Subtracting 1-place numbers 28, 29
    Subtracting 1- and 2-place numbers without regrouping 30, 31
    Subtracting 2 digits without regrouping 32, 33
    Subtracting 2 digits with regrouping 34, 35

MULTIPLICATION AND DIVISION
    Fact families 36, 37
    Multiplication picture problems 38
    Introducing division 39

PROBLEM SOLVING
    Sorting and grouping 40, 44
    Solving story and picture problems 27, 38, 39, 43
    Solving number sentences 41, 42
    Writing simple equations 41, 42

TIME, MONEY, AND MEASUREMENT
    Telling time 45
    Comparing coins and amounts 46, 47, 48
    Comparing lengths 49
    Comparing weights 50
    Introducing perimeter 51

GRAPHS, CHARTS, AND TABLES
    Ordered pairs 52
    Reading and creating simple graphs 53, 54
    Plotting coordinates 20, 23, 29, 32
    Tally counts 44, 54
    Reading charts and tables 10, 44

FRACTIONS
    Identifying parts of a whole 55, 56, 57
    Finding parts of a whole or group 58, 59